Luxe
Vintage

Luxe Vintage

vintage inspired interiors and projects

Tahn Scoon

Photography by John Downs

NEW HOLLAND

Contents

The Handmade and Vintage Home

To slow down, to simplify, these are the things I aspire to. To use only what you need and have room to breathe. Time to potter. This predominately requires an internal shift, but surrounding yourself with only the useful and the beautiful, and organising your home in a way that encourages clutter-free, clean spaces certainly helps. The key to uncluttered spaces of course is to own fewer things and ensure you have adequate storage for the things you do own. It also helps when styling your home to leave white, or breathing, spaces. It relaxes us.

Another way to feel more relaxed at home is to opt for easy-care pieces. Waxed timber floors will show less dirt than white, high-gloss tiles, crushed linen is easier to live with than must-be-ironed crisp cotton and a distressed tabletop is easier to care for than a polished one. Upholster furniture in heavy commercial grade or even outdoor fabrics, or opt for slipcovers you can throw in the wash.

Where practical, try and use as many natural materials around the home as you can. They're more tactile and we seem to prefer the feel, and sometimes even the smell, of them. Natural materials also tend to age much more beautifully than their man-made counterparts. Pilling polyester has nothing on the softness of aged linen and MDF will never develop the coveted patina old timber does. Finishes matter too, so opt for low VOC (volatile organic compounds) paints, glues and sealers. There's not much point having natural timber floors if you are going to cover them in an oil-based polyurethane; try a hardwax oil instead.

Vintage pieces, from a bone china teacup right through to hardwood French doors can add history and beauty in a socially responsible way. Whilst genuine antiques may be prohibitively expensive, vintage encompasses coveted pieces that sit somewhere between everyday second hand and truly antique — and as such, pieces range from the extremely cheap to the extremely cheeky — but bargains can always be found, especially by the astute hunter.

Many vintage pieces are perfect as they are; their faded beauty only enhances their gentle appeal. Some, however, will need a little bit of work. Fabric may need soaking, re-dying or the odd moth hole repaired. Large pieces in good nick are a lucky find and

can be repurposed creatively into any number of household furnishings. Smaller pieces can be stitched together to form patchwork. Furniture can be repainted, restained, reupholstered — or even entirely reinvented.

If you can carve out the time, it's enjoyable to make or repair things with your hands. The trick is to start with small, simple projects and work your way up. Ensure you have all the tools you need and set yourself up in a good spot.

Traditionally almost everything was handmade, and handmade well, out of quality materials. Quite different to today's mass-produced, MDF furniture. You could of course seek out quality contemporary pieces by local artisans, but labour costs are not what they were and in most cases buying vintage will certainly be cheaper. I know of one homeowner who bought six pairs of mismatched, solid timber French doors and painted them all white. He was able to renovate around them to compensate for any minor size discrepancies, and he paid only a small fraction of what it would have cost to commission new hardwood doors.

How many older pieces you introduce into your home is largely dependent on its era and architectural style; an older, character home can be almost exclusively furnished in vintage, whereas a contemporary apartment will only handle a few simple pieces. To tie vintage in with existing newer items, look at line and colour. Fine with fine. Chunky with chunky. And even the most unworkable pieces can be coaxed together by painting them in the same colour.

Opposite page: The vintage wall sconce in this room has been wired to the wall, however the crystal teardrop pendants serve a decorative purpose only, which negates the need for them to be in perfect working order. Removing ornate frames from old artwork can lend a less formal, more relaxed appeal.

TIPS ON CARE OF WALLC

Vintage light fittings can give you real value, as they're often made of materials such as brass and crystal, whereas, similarly priced new lights will most likely be chrome and plastic. Vintage lights are also prettier. To ensure the wiring is still safe, always have old lights checked and installed by a qualified electrician.

Above left: *This beautiful quilt is handmade and looks new but was found in an op shop, so I'm wondering if a kindly soul made it as a donation. Everything else in this picture is a pre-loved find. The old bedhead was rusted to further age its appearance, as can be seen in our project on page 98.*

Left: *Luxe is in the details — custom cushions in Schumacher Sinhala Sky piped in a contrast linen and filled with feather.*

Opposite page: *An antique, Italian-framed tub chair has been reupholstered in sumptuous velvet and its seat cushion refilled with plump feathers. Though the furniture, art and lamp are all vintage finds, the overall scheme is kept light and airy thanks to the generous use of white in the backdrop.*

Opposite page: With the exception of the contemporary artwork, all of the pieces depicted are vintage finds — tied together by a shared colour palette of blue, brown and mustard.

One chair three ways: a vintage slipper chair can be easily and inexpensively updated by simply repainting the legs and adding a slipcover.

Above left: *Original* chair, shabby but sweet.

Above right: *Dressed in a Bianca Lorenne floral.*

Right: *Fresh and* gorgeous in relaxed linen.

A veranda was partially closed in to create this simple but surprisingly luxurious ensuite. The clever homeowner whitewashed the walls, dressed the window and installed DIY shelves — and it was all done incredibly affordably.

Art allows you to contemplate something beautiful as you bathe. Just ensure you don't hang anything too precious though, as there's also a chance of water damage.

Above: There is something perfectly serene about a table dressed in linen and set with classic white fine china. Whilst this vintage Wedgewood tea set wasn't particularly inexpensive, it was still only a fraction of the price of buying new.

Left: When selecting task lighting for an office, keep in mind the light should fall on the task, not the worker. This old banker's light is perfect.

Opposite page: An office can be furnished beautifully but affordably in vintage finds. To promote a sense of calm, a charity store kitchen table and chair have been painted in white. Meanwhile, large inspirational boards contain the visual clutter of paperwork and pictures.

Opposite page: This exquisite antique-inspired bedhead was custom made in a Bianca Lorenne fabric. The dark periwinkle blue of the flowers is picked up in our repainted bedside project — see page 86.

Above left: Star jasmine and butterfly plant have been freshly plucked from the garden and deposited into deliciously makeshift vessels.

Above right: This grand old dame received a revamp via lush new Mokum covers and plump feather inserts.

Right: Look for unusual ways to display everyday items such as napkins and cutlery.

Fabric Projects

If you can learn to sew just a few simple projects, you can really make your home your own and save money. All you need is a beginner's sewing machine — mine even has the 'how to thread' instructions imprinted on it, which is handy as I forget every time — and the skill to sew in a straight line, which is easy to pick up.

We've chosen to use linen for many of the projects in this book as it has such a classic appeal and gets softer and more beautiful with age. It can be quite an expensive fabric to buy today, so it's a surprise to learn it used to be cheaper than cotton and, at one point, all household linens used to be made from linen, hence the term.

We've also used a number of designer remnants, as it's a great way to introduce high-end fabrics into the home without spending too much. Due to the inherent sizes available, remnants work best for smaller projects such as lampshades and pillowslips.

Vintage fabrics are also a great way to make more personalised soft furnishings. You can buy end-of-roll pieces or repurpose old bed linen, curtains or clothes. Sweet, Liberty-style prints are especially pretty in children's rooms.

Sewing tips:
»   All hems are 1.5 cm/½ in unless otherwise specified.
»   Pressing your hems and seams before pinning and sewing really does make sewing easier. In some cases, it even negates the need to pin, so set up an ironing board next to your sewing machine.
»   'Single hem' simply means to fold your hem over once before pressing and sewing. This leaves a raw (or unfinished) edge, which in these projects will end up hidden. However, if your fabric is prone to excessive fraying, you might like to overlock (or run a zigzag stitch) along the raw edge before hemming.
»   To create a 'double hem', fold your hem over twice before pressing and sewing. This will create a neater finish than a single hem.
»   Conversions from metric to imperial are rounded off, as usually the exact measurements don't matter too much. For example, if you want to make a cushion

cover to fit a 50 cm/20 in insert, the made measurement of the cover could be anything from 45 to 55 cm/18 to 22 in. So don't worry about everything being too exact.

» Talking about inserts, ensure you use feather, or at least a feather-mix filling; it'll make your cushions look much more luxurious.

» The following projects are a guideline. Feel free to adjust and redesign in your own vision; it's the most enjoyable part of the creative process.

Tips on selecting and caring for vintage fabrics:

» Only buy natural fabrics, such as cotton, linen and silk. To test if a fabric is natural, scrunch it in your hand. If it leaves creases, it's natural. If it springs out flat, it's most likely a synthetic.

» To remove yellow stains from old fabric, soak in mild detergent and water and then pat dry before applying a stain remover. Make sure the remover contains hydrogen peroxide and not bleach, as it will be much more gentle on delicate old fabrics.

» If old, unused fabric smells musty. Wash twice and line dry in the sun. You might also like to spritz with a homemade linen water before ironing.

LINEN WATER RECIPE

Linen water will give your linens a fresh, summery scent. Try lavender, lemon or orange. Spray linens lightly when ironing, or just after they've been freshly dried in the sun.

What you will need:
2 tablespoons of vodka or witch hazel
20 drops of essential oil
500 ml/18 fl oz spray bottle
Distilled water
Sticky label

What to do:
1. This is exceedingly simple to make; it's just essential oil and water, with a diluter ingredient to help mix the two together. You can use either vodka or witch hazel as the diluter.
2. Start by placing the diluter and oil in the spray bottle and give it a good shake. Once it's combined, fill to about three-quarters full with water and shake again.

No-Zip Cushion with Flange

A no-zip (or 'envelope') cushion is incredibly easy to make for the very reason it has no zip to install. Instead you simply take one piece of fabric and fold it over itself to create a little overlap for the filling to be inserted into.

From there it takes only one more simple step to create a flange (or border), which I think really adds to the cover and makes it look a little fancier than it is. The measurements below are for a standard 50 cm/20 in cushion, however, you can always adjust to make any size you desire.

What you will need:
A piece of fabric cut to 55 x 120 cm/22 x 47 in
Sewing machine and matching thread

What to do:
1. Double hem the two short ends of your fabric.
2. Place right side up and fold the two short ends in towards each other so that they overlap, adjusting until the fabric measures around 50 cm/20 in square.
3. Pin and sew along your two raw edge sides.
4. Turn right side out and use tailor's chalk or pencil to mark out your flange, approximately 2.5 cm/1 in from the edge, and then topstitch. Add a second topstitch in a contrasting colour if you wish.

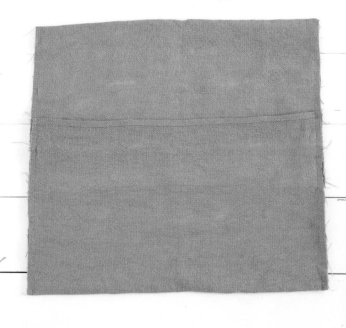

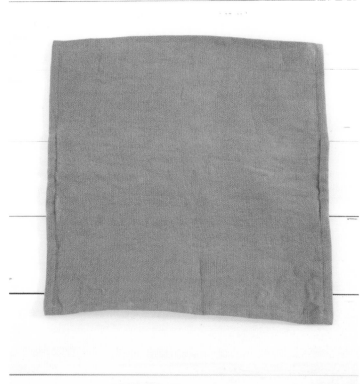

No-Zip Cushion with Ruffle

To add a pretty little ruffle to the back of the cushion, make the cushion as above then make the frill separately before stitching them together. The ruffle not only looks lovely but it also helps hide the opening.

What you will need:
A piece of fabric cut to 15 x 100 cm/6 x 40 in for the ruffle
A piece of fabric cut to 6 x 56 cm/2 x 22 in for the band
Sewing machine and matching thread

What to do:
1. Press and double hem the two short sides and one long side of your ruffle fabric.
2. Sew a long running stitch across the remaining long side of your ruffle fabric, 2 cm/1 in from the edge (don't back stitch after sewing as you won't be able to pull your thread).
3. Gently pull on the bottom thread of your running stitch to create a ruffle 47 cm/18.5 in long. Once you're happy with the gather, tie off the ends and then stitch across the gathering stitch to hold it in place.
4. Press a hem around all four sides of your band fabric. Fold in half lengthways. Press and topstitch the three unfolded sides.
5. Place the ruffle onto the band, right sides together, edge to edge with the ruffle on top of the raw, 'unfinished' edge of the band. The band will be 1.5 cm/0.5 in longer than the ruffle on both sides. Pin and sew.
6. Turn over and press band out flat. Pin band to the top of the finished cushion's opening or 'envelope', right side on right side, and topstitch along the bottom and the top of the band to attach it to the cushion (overlap the band a little by pinning it above your cushion hem to make it easier to sew).

Design details such as borders, boxing and ribbon will make a cushion look more luxe. Also consider trims, ruching and self or contrast piping.

One cushion three ways:

Above left: Boxed cushion.

Above right: Ribboned cushion.

Left: Flanged cushion.

3

5

After

Linen Curtain

For windows that only require a light covering, a simple unlined linen curtain is perfect. It will still allow some light to penetrate but will offer enough privacy when needed. The style is classic and relaxed and the curtain so simple to make.

Please note, if you live in a hot climate and the curtain is exposed to the full sun, natural linen will fade very quickly, so in this case it's best to line your curtain.

What you will need:
A piece of fabric (see step one for how to calculate your measurements)
Sewing machine and matching thread
Embroidery needle and thread for your feature stitch (this can be in the same colour for a subtle effect or in a contrasting colour for something more dramatic)

What to do:
1. Measure your window from the rod to the floor; this is your drop. Add 20 cm/8 in for the channel and hem. The width needs to be at least as wide as your window but can be as much as double the width if a fuller curtain is desired.
2. Press and single hem the top and bottom of your fabric. Press and double hem the two sides of your fabric.
3. Fold the top of your curtain over by around 7 cm/3 in, press and sew. Leave the sides open to create a channel for your rod.
4. Repeat with the bottom to create a hem. Double check the hem length at this point and adjust as necessary.
5. Use either tailor's chalk or even a strip of masking tape to mark out a line across the bottom of your curtain, just above the hem, and then hand stitch a running stitch with your embroidery needle and thread.

Sheer Curtain

Sheer curtains are even lighter than unlined linen and will offer some privacy and gently obscure an unwanted view without hindering the amount of sunlight entering the room. Furthermore, the sunlight will be a little diffused, which cuts down on glare and is always rather pretty.

The light weight of the curtain means it can be easily hung by way of inexpensive spring clips.

What you will need:
A piece of sheer fabric (see step one for how to calculate your measurements)
Sewing machine and matching thread
Spring clips and rings (available from sewing stores)

What to do:
1. Measure your window from the rod to the floor; this is your drop. Add 10 cm/4 in for hems. The width needs to be at least as wide as your window but can be as much as double the width if a fuller curtain is desired.
2. Press, pin and sew a hem around all four sides of your fabric.
3. Check the length and then turn up the bottom of your fabric and hem again.
4. Attach to the rod with your spring clips.

A note on installing rods:
Purchase a rod set, which will include the rod, two brackets and screws. Screw the brackets into the wall and hang the rod. As a general rule of thumb, mount rods 10 cm/4 in (or a hand's width) above and to the sides of the architrave (window frame). You'll need a power drill for some types of walls but plasterboard can be drilled into by hand.

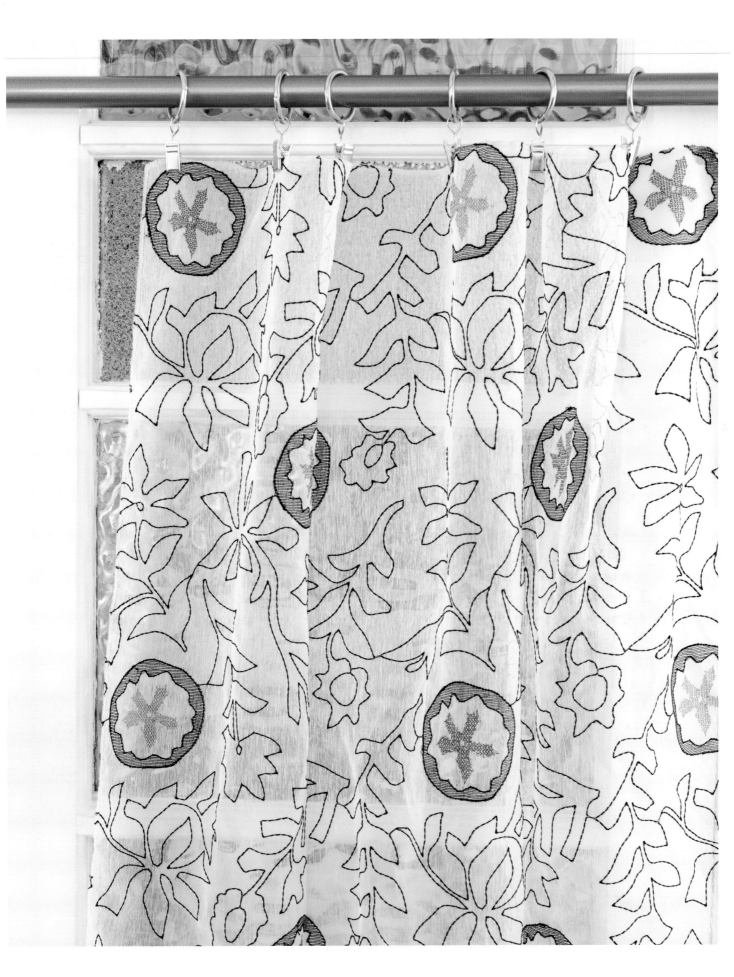

1

2

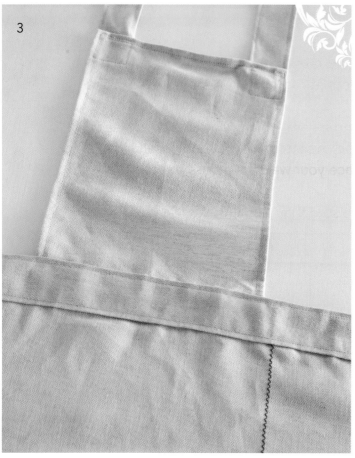

3

After

Apron with Bib

A simple linen apron is classically French and looks good thrown on over anything. We've made this one to fit what we hope is an average size but really, what is that anyway? The main thing is it should be comfortable, so make it fairly generous and at whatever length suits.

What you will need:
A piece of fabric cut to 75 x 95 cm/30 x 37 in for the apron
A piece of fabric cut to 25 x 35 cm/10 x 14 in for the bib
A piece of fabric cut to 15 cm x 200 cm/6 x 79 in for the waist tie
Two pieces of fabric cut to 15 x 80 cm/6 x 31 in each for the neck ties
Sewing machine and matching thread
Red thread for the contrasting topstitch

What to do:
1. Hem along all sides of both your apron and bib fabrics. Use your red thread to run a contrasting zigzag stitch down one side of your apron, approximately a third of the way in from the edge.
2. Make your waist and two neck ties by pressing a hem around all four sides of each tie, fold in half lengthways and then press and topstitch the three unfolded sides.
3. Layer your apron over your bib, and then place your waist tie across the top. Pin and sew.
4. Sew your neck ties onto your apron. To make sure they're secure, topstitch with an 'x' inside a square.

Tea Towel

When I'm working as a magazine stylist, I almost always replace any worn tea towels with fresh, linen ones. It's one of the easiest ways to instantly freshen up a kitchen. The only problem is good quality linen towels can be expensive to buy — so I was rather pleased when I realised how easy it was to whip one up yourself out of any linen remnant.

What you will need:
A piece of fabric 55 x 65 cm/22 x 26 in
Sewing machine and matching thread
Red thread for the contrasting topstitch
A little bit of ribbon or tape (around
   15 cm/6 in)

What to do:
1. Fold your ribbon in half and press.
2. Use your red thread to run a contrasting zigzag stitch from the bottom to the top of your tea towel, around a fifth of the way in.
3. Press and double hem around all four sides of your fabric, with your folded ribbon tucked into one of the hems.

Pillowcase

In more frugal days, the good parts of worn sheets would be saved and turned into smaller items, like pillowcases. You could use your own old sheets for this project, especially expensive ones, as it's a great way to extend their worth. Or you could source vintage sheets from your local charity store. There are plenty floating about in that now obsolete 'double bed' size, which rather fortuitously are about the right width you'll need to make the cases.

Alternatively, a vintage-inspired fabric works beautifully. We've used a sweet Liberty print. The method is the same as in the No-Zip Cushion with Flange, it's just the size of the fabric that is different.

What you will need:
A piece of fabric 57 x 170 cm/22 x 67 in
Sewing machine and matching thread
Buttons (optional)

What to do:
1. Double hem the two short ends of your fabric using a 3 cm/1 in hem (this will provide facing for your buttons should you need it).
2. Place right side up and fold the two short ends in towards each other so that they overlap, adjusting until the fabric measures around 70 cm/28 in in length.
3. Pin and sew along your two raw edge sides.
4. Turn right side out and mark out a 2.5 cm/1 in flange around your entire case. Topstitch.
5. Use the buttonhole setting on your machine to add buttons if you wish. It will help to close the case more securely but it's not 100 per cent necessary.

Please note: this makes a big, bouncy pillowcase measuring around 70 x 50 cm /28 x 20 in, you can make bigger or smaller as needed.

Summer Quilt

There are quite a few vintage sheet sets out there, particularly in double bed sizes. Many are still in their original packets. I can only think they've been languishing away in the back of a warehouse somewhere until recently, when vintage came back into vogue.

The thing is, they didn't used to do fitted sheets, so a sheet set contains two flat sheets, which is perfect for making a light summer quilt — and the double-bed sizes lend themselves well to making quilts for kids' king single or single beds.

What you will need:
A set of two vintage sheets
A piece of wadding cut to the same size
Sewing machine and matching thread
Embroidery needle and thread for hand sewing running stitch

What to do:
1. Layer your three pieces of fabric together with the sheets right sides together and then the wadding placed on top.
2. Pin and sew around three sides, leaving one short side open.
3. Turn right side out. The wadding layer should now be sandwiched between the sheets.
4. Turn under the raw edges of the open end and top stitch closed with your machine.
5. To prevent the layers from billowing (and to look pretty) hand stitch a few lines of running stitches across your quilt, ensuring you sew through all three layers of fabric.

Patchwork Throw

Patchwork came about as a way for women to use up every last scrap of fabric and avoid waste. It's still a thrifty way to turn too-small pieces into something usable. I was lucky enough to be given a discontinued sample book of designer silks, which with a little help from my mum, I made into a lap throw.

Any collection of fabrics, remnants or otherwise, will work. Just remember to make sure all fabrics share the same composition to make washing easier. Traditionally you'd use cotton for quilting but seeing as I was given these silk samples, I've continued with the same fabric and used silk for the backing cloth as well.

What you will need:
12 squares of fabric, all cut to the same size (use a square edge ruler to mark up)
Backing fabric, the same overall size as your squares, but add an extra 10 cm/4 in to each side
Sewing machine and matching thread

What to do:
1. Pin and sew your squares together into four rows of three, and then pin and sew your rows together. Your patchwork front is now complete.
2. Trim your backing fabric so that it is around 10 cm/4 in bigger than your patchwork front on all four sides. Hem along all four sides
3. Place your patchwork fabric on top of your backing fabric, wrong sides together.
4. Fold the edges of the backing fabric over the patchwork along the two long sides. Pin and sew.
5. Now do the same with the two short sides, taking care to tuck the corners in neatly as you go (if you're a more experienced sewer, you may prefer to mitre the corners properly).

A note on cutting squares:
More experienced quilters will use a cutting mat and a rotary blade, which is much quicker, but as it's an investment, if you're only going to make the odd quilt, a square ruler will do just fine.

Fabric Lampshade

If you've never re-covered a lampshade before, start with a drum shade. It's by far the easiest to cover, as the sides are parallel so you don't have to curve your fabric. I picked this shade up from a charity store for just a few dollars and covered it in remnant Catherine Martin fabric. The entire project took less than half an hour and was easier than I expected.

What you will need:
A piece of fabric (see step one for how to calculate your measurements)
Scissors
Spray adhesive suitable for fabric

What to do:
1. Measure the circumference of your shade and add 3 cm/1 in, this is your width. Measure the height of your lampshade and add 4 cm/1.5 in, this is your length. Cut fabric to the correct width and length.
2. It's best to spray outside to avoid any mess, perhaps lay a plastic cloth on an outside table. Lay your fabric out flat, wrong side up. Spray generously, especially around the edges.
3. Fold over on one short end by about 1.5 cm/0.5 in and press down firmly to create a hem.
4. Starting at the raw short edge end, line your lampshade up and roll neatly over the fabric, smoothing as you go. Ensure you roll evenly, leaving a couple of centimetres each side the entire way round.
5. Pop your shade onto its base. This will make it easier to fold over the top and bottom of the shade to stick it down. You may need a little more glue at this stage. Allow to dry.

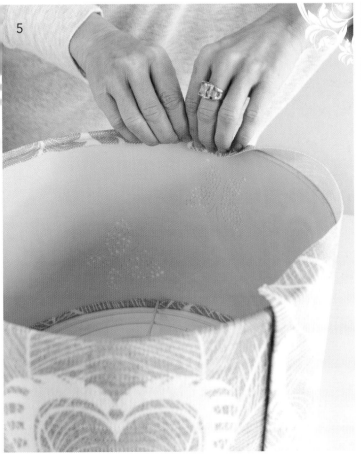

After

Upholstered Bedhead

An upholstered bedhead is superbly comfortable, especially if you like to prop yourself up in bed with a good book. They're also a great way to add colour and pattern, and some much-coveted softness. Whilst they can be quite expensive to buy, they're surprisingly simple to make, in the smaller sizes at least. You do need a nice clear space to work in, a large table is ideal but the floor will do in a pinch.

What you will need:
MDF board (cut to size — see note below on sizing)
5 cm/2 in thick foam cut to the same size as your board
Wadding cut to 10 cm/4 in bigger than your board on all sides
Fabric cut to 10 cm/4 in bigger than your board on all sides
Glue
Staple gun

What to do:
1. Attach the foam to the MDF board with glue.
2. Lay the board, foam side down, onto the wadding. Wrap wadding firmly around the board and staple to the back. It's easiest to start with a staple to the middle of each side and each corner, and then go back around adding more staples. If the wadding is too bulky in the corners, trim with scissors. Trim any excess wadding.
3. Repeat this process with the fabric.

A note on sizing:
Measure the width of your bed and add a couple of centimetres each side, this will be the width of your MDF board. The height of your board will be 90 cm/35 in. This is high enough to be attached to the wall above your bed. Most larger hardware stores will cut MDF to size for you.

Mounting the bedhead:
The easiest way to mount the bedhead is to use keyhole brackets and screws — or a French cleat hanging system — both of which can be found at your local hardware store.

Upholstered Bedhead

Buttoned Upholstered Bedhead

If you'd like to take the above project one step further and add buttons to your bedhead, make the bedhead as above but add the following steps…

What you will need:
Drill
Fabric buttoning kit
Fabric to cover buttons
Darning needle and cord
Staple gun

What to do:
1. Make your bedhead as per the previous instructions but before attaching the foam and wadding, drill 6 to 12 evenly spaced holes into your MDF board (the number of holes is dependent on the size of your bedhead and the look you're after).
2. Cover your buttons with fabric as per the instructions on the pack. You'll need the same number of buttons as holes drilled.
3. Attach the buttons to the covered bedhead with the darning needle and cord. Start at the back of each pre-cut hole and push the darning needle through to sew on the button. Once your button is on, tie off at the back and secure with a couple of staples.

Wall and Wallpaper
Projects

Walls can make a huge impact on your overall decorating scheme. In general, fresh white walls are the easiest to work with, especially when incorporating vintage pieces. However, when more impact is needed, play with colour or introduce wallpaper.

Don't think of the horribly coloured psychedelic papers of the seventies, instead think of the gorgeously decadent designs of the roaring twenties, or the romantic prints uncovered and rediscovered in old Parisian apartments.

If you're fortunate enough to find a roll or two of vintage paper, it will look amazingly sweet in a little girl's room, especially teamed with fresh white furniture. In most cases, you'll be hard pressed to find enough vintage rolls to cover a room in its entirety, however you can always do a feature wall or even half walls if you're lucky enough to have picture or dado rails.

Old papers are a little trickier to get up, and take down than the new non-woven papers we have today — however, it's still worth the effort due to their considerable charm.

How to Paint Walls

What you will need:
Sugar soap
Cloth
Drop sheets
Masking tape
Undercoat (optional)
Low-sheen acrylic paint
Paint brush
Roller and roller tray

What to do:
1. Clean walls thoroughly with sugar soap and a cloth and allow to dry.
2. Drag furniture into the middle of the room and cover with drop sheets. Apply masking tape to light fittings, power outlets and along skirtings and trims. Cover the floor with drop sheets.
3. Apply one coat of undercoat to seal and prime walls (in much the same way as you might apply a primer to your face). This step must be taken if walls are raw or in poor condition — however, you can skip this step if walls are already painted and in reasonable condition.
4. Apply the first coat of paint. Use a paint brush to cut in along the edges, cornices and skirtings before using the roller to fill in the main part of the wall.
5. Allow the first coat to dry before applying a second coat.

'I believe in optimism and plenty of white paint.' Elsie de Wolfe

TIPS FOR PAINTING WALLS

* *For your own health and the health of the environment, use low VOC water-based paints. Water-based paints are also easier to clean up.*
* *If you're looking to add colour to your walls, in my opinion, the natural paint companies have better colour palettes. This is because they use natural pigments rather than synthetic. It gives the colours an earthy, more authentic hue.*
* *Buy special removable masking tape from a paint shop — it's very disheartening if you leave regular masking tape on too long and it leaves a mess when you take it off.*
* *Buy good quality brushes. Cheaper brushes tend to lose more bristles — which is not a good look on your walls.*
* *Dip no more than a third of your brush into the paint. Gently wipe or tap excess paint back into the tin.*
* *'Cutting in' with the brush before using the roller, gives the roller a little edge to work within, which prevents you accidentally painting the skirtings etc.*
* *When using the roller, keep the edges wet to avoid overlap marks.*

TIPS FOR CLEANING UP

* *If you've been painting with water-based paints, you can rinse brushes, rollers and trays in the sink but avoid rinsing over outside drains as they generally run directly into waterways.*
* *If you have leftover paint the best way to dispose of it is to offer it to someone else who may need it. If you're unable to give it away, don't pour it down the drain as most councils won't allow it. Instead use kitty litter or sand to solidify the paint before disposing of it in the bin.*

New Non-Woven Wallpaper

The new, non-woven wallpapers commonly available today are much easier to install, and remove, than their vintage counterparts. The main reason being you paste the walls rather than the paper — this is a much more forgiving process. Having said that, there's still an art to it and so if you're using very expensive paper and there are a lot of obstacles to negotiate, such as light fittings or plumbing, call in an expert.

However, if the wallpaper isn't hugely expensive and it's a simple, straightforward wall such as a feature wall in a bedroom, it's not too hard to do yourself. The trick is to set yourself up with the right equipment, including a large table to cut on, and ensure you prep your walls well.

Prepping your walls
»   If your walls are new and constructed from bare gyprock, seal the surface with a wallboard sealer. If the walls are painted with acrylic paint, simply sand lightly.
»   Apply a coat of size to the wall (available from hardware stores). The role of size is to help even up the porosity of the wall, giving you a smoother finish — it also gives a little bit of slip, allowing you to more easily slide the wallpaper sideways when lining up pattern.

TIPS ON CALCULATING HOW MANY ROLLS YOU WILL NEED
*   *Measure your wall from top to bottom, this is your drop. Most wallpapers come in 53 cm/21 in wide rolls, so you need to then measure how many times 53 cm fits across the width of your wall and multiply it by your drop measurement. Then as most rolls come in lengths of 10 m/33 ft, you can then calculate how many rolls you need.*
*   *If the above seems too convoluted, simply find an online wallpaper calculator and fill it in; you'll have the answer in seconds.*
*   *If you have a patterned paper, always allow a little extra for the pattern repeat.*

How to Hang New (Non-Woven) Wallpaper

What you will need:

Wallpaper (see note on measuring up)

Tape measure and scissors

Wallpaper paste

Roller

Straight edge spreader (a plastic tool that helps smooth the paper)

Sharp knife and ruler (the ruler needs to be longer than the width of the paper and preferably with a handle)

What to do:

1. Measure your drop and cut wallpaper to length, being careful to match your pattern repeats, and allowing a little extra for overhang (which will be trimmed off later).

2. Mix the paste as per instructions on the pack and apply to wall with a roller. Cut into the wall (with a brush held sideways) as required (and don't worry if you get some glue on the cornice or ceiling, you can just wipe it off with a rag after you've trimmed your paper later).

3. Hang your drops of wallpaper from the top to the bottom of the wall, smoothing the paper out with a straight edge spreader as you go.

4. Trim paper along the top and the bottom with a sharp knife or blade and a ruler. Repeat until the wall is done.

HOW TO HANG VINTAGE WALLPAPER

Follow the instructions for non-woven paper, with the major exception of pasting the paper instead of the walls. This is a little messier perhaps but made much easier if you ensure you have a big table to work from.

Wallpaper House Mural

We used vintage wallpaper found in a charity store to create this playhouse-shaped mural, which looks particularly sweet in a children's playroom. We were lucky that we could line our pieces up against the tongue and groove walls, however, if you have plasterboard walls, simply check your first piece with a spirit level and work out from there.

The shape is superbly easy to make, it's simply two or three drops of wallpaper to create the base of the house and then two triangular pieces to form the roof. An old frame is used to create the illusion of a front door and rectangles of contrasting wallpaper for the windows.

As we used vintage paper, we had to glue the paper rather than the wall (a couple of extra drawing pins helped).

Wallpaper Butterflies

For little leftover bits of wallpaper, use a butterfly (or other) shaped cookie cutter to trace your shapes, cut out and fold lightly to create an impression of movement.

Butterflies can be made into bunting, mobiles or used as decorations on homemade greeting cards.

Wallpaper Chains

Another sweet way to use up those little leftover bits of wallpaper is to make a paper chain. Simply cut out small rectangular strips of paper of the same size. Make your first loop by gluing the ends of one strip together, then thread through your next strip and keep looping and gluing until your chain is formed.

Chains can be made in Christmas colours and strung on your tree or simply used as a pretty vintage decoration in a child's room.

Wallpapered Stairs

Stairways are such utilitarian spaces, and as such they're often under-decorated. Adding art and dramatic lighting can help enormously but another less common option is to wallpaper your risers.

Vintage papers work well in character homes, whilst contemporary papers are more suited to newer homes. You can wallpaper the entire riser, or just create a 'runner' as we have done. In this older home the stairs are relatively narrow so we were able to make the runner the width of the roll, which was rather lucky. To ensure your paper will be centered correctly, measure the width of your stairs and mark your in and out points with chalk.

What you will need:
Wallpaper
Tape measure
Metal ruler and pencil
Scissors or craft knife
Wallpaper glue

What to do:
1. Give your stair risers a quick clean and allow to dry.
2. Measure the height of your risers.
3. Use your ruler and pencil to measure and mark the back of your wallpaper before cutting into strips.
4. Apply your glue (to the paper if using vintage wallpaper, to the risers if using new).
5. Press into position, smoothing out towards the edges as you go.

Furniture Projects

Gorgeous old, solid-timber pieces are easy to source affordably and are generally fairly easy to update with paint, stain or fabric. The trick is to ensure you love the shape, as that won't change, and check the structure is sound. A drawer that sticks a little can be coaxed to run smoothly with a little wax but runners that are beyond repair may be too time consuming and expensive to replace.

Also, make sure you're not about to paint over a genuine antique, as you may severely depreciate its value. Having said that, I do sometimes encourage clients to refinish heavy antique pieces in a contemporary high-gloss paint, but only with full disclosure that it will be expensive to reverse. Some clients are happy to do this as the antique finish may be too dark for their new home but they still want to keep the piece for financial or sentimental reasons.

When you're dealing with newer, everyday vintage pieces though, you can be as daring as you like with your choices, as you're more likely to be adding value. Paint, in particular, is such a forgiving medium; even if everything goes horribly wrong you can always sand it back and start again.

The only other thing to consider before you start revamping old furniture is lead paint. You obviously want to avoid sanding it back as the dust is harmful. It was phased out in the 1970s so it's only a concern if the piece is older than that. If you're unsure, buy a lead paint testing kit from your local hardware store. They're extremely cheap and very easy to use. If your piece does contain lead paint, take the proper precautions or pass the project on to a professional. Most of the time, however, your piece won't be old enough to worry about and you can sand away freely — though it's still prudent to wear a dust mask and sand outdoors.

When it comes time to paint I always prefer using products from the natural paint companies where possible. The paints are coloured with natural pigments so have a soft, earthy tone to them — and as they're extremely low VOC (volatile organic compounds) they're healthier to work with and don't emit that unpleasant 'paint' smell.

How to Paint Timber Furniture

Most timber pieces can be made over quickly and easily with a couple of coats of paint. Generally, this is a simple, three-step process that only takes an afternoon or two. Set yourself up in a nice spot in the garden, with a drop sheet and all your painting equipment (and perhaps a little Vivaldi playing in the background to make it even more enjoyable).

For most furniture projects, a satin finish works well as it gives a mid-level gloss — hardier than a matte finish but more forgiving of fingerprints than high-gloss.

What you will need:
Warm damp cloth
Sandpaper
Acrylic paint in satin

What to do:
1. Clean your furniture thoroughly with a warm, damp cloth. Allow to dry.
2. Sand back until smooth and then wipe away any dust.
3. Apply two coats of paint. Allow for plenty of drying time between coats.

EXTRA PAINTING TIPS

* *Remove any hardware such as handles and hinges if you don't want paint on them (we didn't worry with this project as the hardware had already been painted over previously) and protect any fixed fittings with masking tape.*

* *In these projects, we've sanded rather than stripped furniture. This is because I don't like the heavy chemicals used in most commercial paint strippers. For most pieces, sanding is easier and less messy. However, if you have an old piece with intricate mouldings, it is better to use a stripper as you may wear away the detail if you sand too vigorously.*

* *Use the right size brush. Small brushes for small pieces, large for large.*

* *The glossier the finish, the hardier it will be. A satin finish will suit most items but high gloss will be more suitable for hard working items such as kitchen tables. Matte finishes are best for more decorative pieces.*

2

2b

3

After

3

4

6

After

How to Age' Timber Furniture

To create an 'aged' paint finish is a simple process that requires a base and top coat in two different colours. The top coat is rubbed back to reveal a little of the base colour, which creates the impression it's worn over time. For a more authentic look, ensure you rub back the top coat in the places where it would naturally receive the most wear and tear, which is predominately the edges.

You can use regular acrylic paint for this project but we've chosen to use chalk paint as its matte, chalky finish is conducive to creating an aged appearance. It also sticks to almost anything, so requires little-to-no prep — and the drying time is incredibly fast so you don't have to wait long between coats. The only downside is the matte finish will mark easily, so you must seal with a wax or acrylic sealer. We used beeswax.

What you will need:
Warm damp cloth
Sandpaper (if needed)
Chalk paint in your chosen base colour
Chalk paint in your chosen top colour
Beeswax and a soft cloth

What to do:
1. Thoroughly clean your furniture.
2. If there are any obvious bumps or flakes, lightly sand and wipe clean — otherwise you can skip this step.
3. Apply one or two coats of your base colour and allow to dry.
4. Apply one coat of your top colour and allow to dry.
5. Lightly sand back the top coat in selected spots to reveal the base colour.
6. Apply a small amount of beeswax with a soft, clean cloth (an old t-shirt is perfect), wiping off any excess as you go.

How to Restain Timber Furniture

Restaining timber furniture is much more time consuming than repainting as you can't just rough up the existing finish as you can for paint, you have to thoroughly remove it or the new stain won't be able to penetrate the wood.

This little old bedside was finished in a pine-coloured timber and had a country-style timber knob. A new walnut stain and a crystal-style knob give it a more elegant and vintage appeal.

What you will need:
Fine hand saw
Screwdriver
Sandpaper
Wood stain
Paint brush
Furniture wax
Drill and drill bits
New crystal-style knob

What to do:
1. Use your handsaw to remove the wooden knob and your screwdriver to remove the hinges and catches, and to allow the door to come away.
2. Sand the cabinet and door, always working with the grain to avoid scratching it. Start with a medium grit paper then finish with a fine grit paper. Dust clean.
3. Apply stain evenly with a clean rag and allow to dry.
4. Apply your furniture wax.
5. Use a pencil to mark where the new knob is to go. Drill your hole and screw your knob into position.
6. Reattach the door to the bedside.

How to Revive and Wax Timber Furniture

If you find a timber piece that is dusty, dirty and dull — but is structurally sound and the colour is good — you don't have to completely strip back and restain. Save time by giving it a quick revive and wax instead.

What you will need:
Small craft knife
Furniture reviver
Fine grade (0000) steel wool
Soft cloths
Toothbrush
Black furniture wax
Gloves

What to do:
1. Use a small craft knife to gently scrape off any lumps of dirt (or more likely, spider droppings). Be very careful not to cut through the finish.
2. Apply the reviver with the fine grade steel wool. It's important to follow the grain so you don't scratch the timber. Keep your strokes long and even. Use the reviver sparingly and wipe off any excess as you go with a soft cloth.
3. If your piece has any intricately carved or moulded areas, work the reviver into them with a toothbrush, working in a circular motion.
4. Apply the wax sparingly with the steel wool (the more you put on, the more you'll have to take off). Wear gloves to protect your hands and to prevent your nails being stained black.
5. Leave to dry for approximately 10 minutes.
6. Burnish off with a soft clean rag (an old t-shirt is perfect).

A note on burnishing:
Burnishing just means to polish — the idea is to rub quite fast so the wax heats up and softens as you work. This process can be repeated many times until you're happy with the result. Allow the wax to dry for around an hour between coats.

How to Paint Metal Furniture

The best way to paint metal furniture is to use an enamel spray paint. This is not the healthiest or most environmental of options I'm afraid, but it will give you the best results. It's important to work in a well-ventilated area, preferably outdoors on a still day, and to wear a mask, safety glasses and gloves. You'll also need a large drop sheet to protect the ground.

This inexpensive metal folding table was stained and well past its prime. It was given a fresh new look with a lick of paint.

What you will need:
Metal brush and sandpaper (if needed)
Warm, soapy water and cloth
Spray can of metal primer
Spray can of enamel paint

What to do:
1. If there is any rust or chipped paint on your piece, brush it down with a metal brush and lightly sand.
2. Wash your piece with warm, soapy water and a cloth. Allow to dry.
3. Apply your metal primer. Ensure you hold the can at least 15 cm/6 in away from your furniture and spray evenly. Allow to dry.
4. Apply two coats of your spray enamel in much the same way. Allow ample drying time between coats.

Please note: Some brands sell enamel spray paints that contain a primer. In this case, you can skip the priming step.

How to Age Metal Furniture

Some of the natural paint companies sell products that will rust almost any interior or exterior surface to create a rusted metal effect. This means you can buy affordable stock standard pieces and make them over to emulate expensive aged items.

This process authentically rusts pieces, so ironically it can't be used on outdoor metal furniture, as it will continue to rust. You can use it on metal furniture inside but it's important to seal it very well to prevent rust from rubbing off.

Interior furniture made from almost any material, non-metal garden furniture, plant pots and picture frames all make for good projects.

We used Murobond Rust Paint, however each company has its own system, so if buying elsewhere read instructions carefully.

What you will need:
Rust paint base
Rust paint finish
Rust paint clear
Brushes
Spray bottle filled with water

What to do:
1. Prepare your surface as per paint manufacturer's instructions.
2. Apply a generous coat of Rust paint base and allow to dry for 3 to 6 hours. Apply a second coat but only allow to partially dry (usually this will be less than 30 minutes).
3. Apply a generous coat of Rust paint finish by brush, laying it on rather than brushing it in. The surface needs to be kept wet for at least 30 minutes, so spray with a fine mist of water as needed. Your furniture should be starting to rust.
4. Once you're happy with the level of rust, apply one or two coats of Rust paint clear to stop the rusting process. This will also provide a clear seal to prevent the rust from rubbing off — and it'll leave you with a washable finish.

Please note: These are the condensed instructions, please read the manufacturer's product data sheet for the full instructions.

Little Ones

Vintage-inspired interiors work so well in children's rooms. Even those pieces that would be too blatantly 'cutesy' for anywhere else in the house can work in a child's bedroom, particularly a little girl's room. From old furniture to over-the-top wallpapers, vintage pieces can add something more authentically unique — again, just ensure you leave some 'white spaces' to prevent the look from becoming overwhelming.

Probably the only other thing to remember is that some more practical items, such as cots and bassinets, won't come up to current safety standards and can only be used decoratively. Most other pieces are fine though. Update where appropriate; timber furniture can be freshened with a coat of paint, vintage curtains resized and old linen repurposed.

It's not only furniture and fabrics though; vintage books and toys can also connect children to the past and bring a lot of joy. Well, Enid Blyton books bring me joy anyway, even if you do have to slightly edit out the blatant sexism as you read aloud to youngsters. And whilst I'd never suggest buying anything in the least unhygienic or unsafe second hand, items such as unpainted timber toys and dress up clothes are perfect.

When vintage shopping and making for children's rooms, preselect a colour palette so all your items work together harmoniously in the end. A colour palette can be a few very specific colours, or a tone of colour, such as gelato, primary or pastel.

Vintage shopping ideas for children
» Dress up clothes can be found for a song, from vintage nighties and dresses to costume tiaras, newsboy caps and superhero capes — wash thoroughly and store in an easily accessible box or bin.
» Vintage books — a much-loved series will look particularly good displayed and can be fun to collect over time.
» Timber furniture and toys, including rockers, pedal cars, doll's beds and table and chair sets. Check the old paint is lead free before stripping and repainting in your favourite hue.

- » Old comic books are enjoyable to read but some of the covers can also look great framed — or use double pages as colourfully quirky gift-wrapping paper.
- » Ornate old frames can be sourced relatively cheaply — you can replace unwanted art with a child's own artwork or paint over it with chalkboard paint to create a 'posh' blackboard.
- » Clothes that fit — whilst old, stained items are not in the least desirable, some pieces improve with age, such as a pair of fashionably faded and worn-in denim jeans.
- » Clothes that don't fit (but are made from fabulous old fabrics, such as an original Liberty print) can be resized or cut up and remade into headscarfs, skirts, bunting or even a patchwork quilt.
- » You can pick up sewing notions (supplies and accessories like pin cushions, seam rippers, buttons and hooks) and remnant fabric for next to nothing. Collect together a simple sewing kit and have fun teaching your little one to sew.

Healthier rooms for children

- » Ensure rooms receive an abundance of fresh air and light to help promote good air quality and prevent mould and dust mites.
- » Keep rooms clean for the same reasons, preferably using non-chemical cleaners. Try a vinegar and warm water mix for mirrors and windows, a soapy damp cloth for general surfaces and invest in a good vacuum cleaner.
- » New MDF (fibreboard) and upholstered furniture can contain glues and finishes that release small amounts of chemicals into the air. Source new eco-friendly, non-toxic pieces instead — or buy quality second-hand, as any chemicals would have already off-gassed.
- » Whilst natural wool is preferable over synthetic carpet, for children with allergies, it's best to avoid carpet altogether. Hard floors are easier to keep free from dust mites and other irritants — and can be strewn with small, easy-to-wash cotton rugs.
- » A good night's sleep is essential for good health, so ensure you fit heavy block out curtains. Stain-resistant synthetic fabrics, however, will introduce chemicals into your child's room, so opt for natural cotton instead.
- » When painting walls and furniture, source no or low VOC (volatile organic compound) paints from natural paint companies to help retain good air quality.

Glitter Playdough Recipe

Less expensive (and less smelly) than bought playdough, the homemade variety can be made in minutes and customised to any colour.

What you will need:
2 cups of plain flour
2 cups of water
1 cup of salt
4 tbsp cream of tartar
2 tbsp cooking oil
Food colouring
Chunky glitter

What to do:
1. Place all the ingredients, aside from the glitter, into a saucepan and stir over a low heat until a dough begins to form. Remove from heat and allow to cool.
2. Once cool, turn it out and knead until smooth.
3. Sprinkle liberally with glitter and knead through.
4. Store in an airtight container.

TIPS
If after time the dough starts to dry out, knead through a couple of drops of water. Conversely, if you live somewhere humid and the dough becomes too moist, try reheating for a few minutes.

Above left: A pale pink vintage tablecloth makes for a pretty bed cover. The handmade cotton, crochet blanket was also a charity store find.

Above right: The cover of this old book has been recently made over with a rather delightful image of a little girl. Rather surprisingly, the book in question is a 1958 edition of The Guns of Navarone.

Left: A vintage toy sewing machine found in a second-hand store sadly no longer sews but children are drawn to its movable wheel anyway. The old thread is very fragile but still intact.

Opposite page: I was delighted to find this seventies pillowslip and bedcover depicting one of my most beloved early childhood characters, Holly Hobbie.

Opposite page and bottom right: From vintage nighties to old dance costumes, cowboy hats, waistcoats, costume jewellery and sparkly socks — op shops are a treasure trove when it comes to collecting for a dress-up box.

Above left: Scraps of pretty fabric can be quickly sewn up into simple bags and used for any number of things, including hair ribbons, sewing notions or pointe shoes.

Above right: A drop of Christian Fischbacher's toile du Jouy inspired 'Liaison' fabric depicts modern and traditional scenes.

Most small children are quite fascinated by a button collection and will happily sort through them, selecting their favourites, for hours. The vintage wallpaper was found in a charity store for only a few dollars.

The timber toy ironing board in this picture was handmade by this little girl's great-grandfather and has been lovingly passed down through the generations. A selection of mismatched vintage linen makes for a pretty 'ironing pile'.

Above left: Vintage children's books are an utter pleasure. Usually wordier than their modern counterparts, they are often beautifully illustrated and, rather delightfully, not at all politically correct.

Above right: Vintage sporting illustrations were the inspiration behind this new, digitally produced wallpaper, custom made for a young cricket lover.

Left: It can be hard to find really gorgeous fabrics for boys' rooms, but classic French ticking always works a treat.

Opposite page: A vintage, 1950s doll pram and a decidedly contemporary art pieces by artist Lisa Taylor King work beautifully together thanks to a shared colour palette.

The Vintage Garden

If you can, it's nice to create at least one little seating nook outside, somewhere you can escape to for a little peace and quiet or perhaps catch a little sun. Though I've never been a huge fan of retro vintage inside the home, I adore it outside. Those sweet little white, filigree chairs dressed in florals and fringed umbrellas in sunshine colours. Whatever your taste, vintage garden furniture is easy to make over.

Old furniture can be primed and repainted and the cushions recovered or replaced. If they need to be replaced, simply measure up and your local foam rubber store can cut to size. Remember to ask for outdoor foam and team with outdoor fabric for longevity.

A garden of course needs greenery. The edible kind does double duty but intersperse flowers too, both for cutting and fragrance. If you're clever you can also add plants that deter unwanted insects; try tansy and mint to repel ants and the herb rue to keep flies and mosquitos at bay.

How to Age Terracotta Pots

A lived-in garden is infinitely more appealing, and one way to create the impression a garden has been around for some time is to 'age' the pots.

Terracotta pots naturally whiten with time but you can age them instantly with the help of a little bit of white paint. Ensure you use a low-VOC paint, especially if you're planning to grow herbs in your pots.

What you will need:
Terracotta pot
White paint
Paint brush and sandpaper

What to do:
1. Clean your pot thoroughly.
2. Water down your paint so it's around one-third paint, two-thirds water.
3. Paint the outside of the pot — you don't have to be neat, random strokes will look better.
4. Lightly sand back until you get the effect you desire.

How to Create Vintage Metal Pots

Almost any old metal container can be turned into a garden pot. Old tea tins can be planted with your favourite herbal teas; a vintage baby's bath can house a kitchen garden or an old watering can some herbs.

The only thing that you need to do is create holes for drainage. This can be done quickly and easily with a hammer and an inexpensive little tool called a centre punch, which helps to pierce the metal safely.

What you need:
Metal container of your choice
Centre punch
Hammer

What to do:
1. Wash your container thoroughly.
2. Turn it upside down and use the hammer and centre punch to hammer holes into the bottom of the container.

How to Pot Herbs

Potted herbs take up very little room — they can be placed in a courtyard, on a balcony or even a sunny kitchen windowsill. They're easy to plant and look after and are a blessing to have close by when cooking. One of my most favourite things is to be able to break off some fresh Italian parsley to sprinkle over scrambled eggs.

Aside from herbs used to flavour food, if you're a tea drinker you might want to include herbs such as mint that can be freshly plucked and steeped in boiling water whenever you need a soothing brew.

What you will need:
Pots
Pebbles
Seedlings
Potting mix
Watering can
Garden gloves

What to do:
1. Thoroughly clean your pot.
2. Add a layer of pebbles to ensure good drainage and help prevent the soil running out of the drainage holes.
3. Fill your pot about three-quarters full with potting mix.
4. Gently add your seedlings and then pack down with a little extra potting mix.
5. Sprinkle with water.

2

4

5

After

TIPS FOR GROWING HERBS

* Aside from pots with good drainage, the other thing herbs need is plenty of sun, especially morning sun. Pots on castors can be a good way to move herbs around to catch the light. Also, they need nutritious soil, so use a good quality, organic mix specifically formulated for edible plants.

* Different herbs will require different levels of watering. As a general rule of thumb, water once a day in summer and two or three times a week in winter. Feed sparingly with an organic liquid fertiliser once every few weeks.

* Many herbs will grow happily together in the same pot, providing it is big enough. However, mint in particular has a tendency to run wild and take over, so it's best to plant out in its own pot. Parsley will happily share pots with anyone.

* Pick herbs regularly as it encourages growth — but pick from the top only so you get a nice short, bushy plant not a tall, slender one.

* Any pickings that you don't use straight away can be stored in the fridge in a glass of water or an airtight container for a few days. To keep herbs longer, chop finely and place in an ice tray with a little bit of water and pop in your freezer. Once frozen you can store your frozen cubes in an airtight container in the freezer.

How to Create a Kitchen Garden

As your existing garden soil may not be suited to growing vegetables, install a raised garden bed, and then fill with a good quality organic soil specifically formulated for edible plants. Raised beds also allow for better drainage, which is important. You can build a permanent border out of timber, rocks or other materials. Buy a pre-made, raised garden bed or create a simple bed from any number of vintage containers.

What you will need:
Good quality garden soil suitable for vegetables
Compost
Organic mulch (lucerne is good)
Seedlings
Trowel, fork, gloves and watering can
Fertiliser (fish emulsion is good)

What to do:
1. Add soil to the garden bed. Healthy soil equals healthy plants, so buy the best you can afford.
2. Mix some good quality compost through the soil (you need around one-third compost to two-thirds soil).
3. Spread with a thin layer of organic mulch to help keep the soil moist.
4. Plant your seedlings in rows, allow for spacing.
5. Water well. Feed regularly with fertiliser.

Five easy-to-grow herbs
»   Basil
»   Mint
»   Parsley
»   Rosemary
»   Thyme

Five easy-to-grow vegetables
»   Beans
»   Beetroot
»   Capsicum
»   Lettuce
»   Tomatoes

Above: This homeowner has cleverly concealed the pool fence behind the veranda balustrade, creating a luxuriously serene landscape.

Above: There are many simple-to-use products that can be applied to metal garden furniture to protect it from rusting — however, there's a certain timeworn appeal in letting nature take its course.

KITCHEN GARDEN TIPS

* If you're placing your kitchen garden border directly onto your lawn, put down a layer of damp newspaper first to suppress weed growth.
* It's important to water your garden regularly, but be careful not to over water. You can test whether your garden needs watering or not by poking your finger into the soil. Ideally the soil needs to be damp, not wet and not dry. It's always best to water your plants first thing in the morning.
* Regularly feed your plants with a little fish emulsion or another quality fertiliser.
* Just a few vegies, a few herbs and a lemon tree are enough to make a substantial difference to the way you eat. If your garden isn't big enough for a lemon tree, try planting one of the dwarf varieties in a pot.
* Scatter some lavender and marigolds through your garden, they'll help keep pests at bay.

Above left: A little summerhouse nestled at the bottom of a hinterland garden offers a welcome retreat from the heat.

Above right: A potting shed wall is adorned with rustic vintage finds.

Opposite page: An inspiring private garden located in a picturesque hinterland mountain village. Also pages 122 and 123.

Afternoon Tea

Afternoon Tea

For those of us who much prefer baking over cooking, afternoon tea is such an easy way to entertain. There's something so meditative about mixing the wet ingredients in with the dry, I'm not sure what it is but I find it extraordinarily relaxing. Also, you can make the table so much prettier with fine china pots and sweet treats.

Though charity stores seemed to have recently cottoned on to the popularity of vintage and have raised their prices accordingly, you can still pick up genuine, fine bone china at a reasonable price, especially if you're happy to mix and match your sets. To check the quality of a piece, hold it up to the light and place your hand behind it. If you can see your hand through the china, it is indeed a fine china.

In much the same way, you can test the authenticity of crystal, as opposed to cut glass, by gently flicking the rim. Crystal will emit a lovely ringing sound. Collect some ornate vintage silverware too. Real silver is the most prestigious, followed by plated and then EPNS. However, I prefer EPNS as it hardly ever needs polishing and seems to survive the dishwasher quite well — whereas real silver needs to be hand washed and polished regularly.

VINTAGE NOTE

Spode was one of the first companies to add animal bone ash to their china recipe back in the early 1800s. The inclusion of bone ash produced the lightest and most translucent, yet durable, china ever made. The delicate beauty of bone china makes it hard to believe it's in fact quite strong and breaks and chips far less easily than inferior china, which is perhaps why many pieces are still around today.

The Perfect Pot

There's an art to making the perfect pot of tea. The most of important thing of course is to use loose-leaf teas, not bags (and I'm not just trying to sound posh, they really do taste different!). I'm also convinced that tea tastes better sipped from a fine china cup. Everyone has their blend of choice, mine is definitely the delicately flower-infused Earl and Lady Greys.

Method:
1. Fill a kettle with cold water and bring to the boil.
2. Tip a little of the boiling water into the teapot and give it a swirl before tipping out.
3. Add one generous teaspoon of tea-leaves per person to the pot.
4. Allow to brew for 5 minutes.
5. If you prefer your tea black, serve with a slice of lemon instead of milk.

If you're serving green tea, the leaves are more delicate, so to prevent it from tasting bitter pour the water in just before it reaches the boil and only steep for a couple of minutes. Green tea should not be served with milk.

Iced Tea

In warmer weather, you may prefer to serve iced tea. Making your own is very easy, and very likely much healthier, than buying pre-made. Iced tea can be made from caffeinated or herbal teas, or a mixture of both, depending on your preference, and sweetened with honey or sugar.

Ingredients:
4 cups of boiling water
4 tea bags
Honey or sugar to taste

Method:
1. Place teabags and honey or sugar in a heatproof pot or bowl and pour in the boiling water.
2. Allow to steep for 5–15 minutes (depending of which tea you use — green tea only needs a few minutes whereas black or herbal will need longer). Remove tea bags and allow to cool.
3. Once cool, transfer into a clean, glass bottle and refrigerate.

Tip: If using a berry tea, such as raspberry and cranberry, try sweetening with jam rather than sugar. It tastes delicious and adds to the colour.

Dainty Sandwiches

Dainty sandwiches is a rather old-fashioned term for little sandwiches cut into triangles. Usually you'd cut the crusts off but as this bread was deliciously fresh, we left them on. To make the sandwiches look prettier and less prosaic, we decorated them by running the herbs along one edge.

There are plenty of filling combinations you can use that incorporate herbs including: chicken, mayo and chives; salmon, cream cheese and chives; and chicken, pesto and basil.

Ingredients:
Free range eggs
Butter
A splash of milk
Salt and pepper
Freshly baked or bought
  bread
Chives, finely chopped

Method:
1. Boil your eggs so they are firm but not hard.
2. Mash a generous amount of butter and a little milk into the eggs, and flavour with salt and pepper.
3. Butter your bread well before filling with the egg mix.
4. Cut into triangles.
5. Place your finely chopped chives onto a plate and roll one edge of your sandwich into the mix to coat it.

Carrot Cake Cookies

Delicious and nutritious, carrot cake cookies are little cakes in a convenient biscuit size. You can serve as is, or you could add 75 g/2.5 oz of cream cheese mixed with 50 g/1.5 oz of butter and 90 g/3 oz of icing sugar (powdered sugar) to make a filling, which can be sandwiched between two cookies. Alternatively, just make a plain glace icing like we did and drizzle over the top.

Ingredients:

250 g/8 oz butter, softened
160 g/5 oz brown sugar
2 free-range eggs, lightly beaten
225 g/7 oz self-raising flour, sifted
½ teaspoon baking powder
1 teaspoon ground cinnamon
190 g/6 oz rolled oats
1 ½ cups grated carrot
½ cup sultanas

Method:

1. Preheat oven to 180°C/350°F.
2. Beat butter and sugar until light and creamy. Add eggs and beat well.
3. Stir in the flour, baking powder and cinnamon.
4. Add oats, carrots and sultanas and mix well.
5. Cover and refrigerate for 30 minutes.
6. Roll tablespoons of mixture into balls and place onto a greased tray 5 cm/2 in apart.
7. Bake in the oven for 10–15 minutes or until lightly browned. Allow to cool on a wire rack.

For Glace Icing:

225 g/8 oz icing sugar (powdered sugar)
2 to 3 tablespoons of boiling water
Squeeze of lemon juice

To Make Glace Icing:

1. Simply mix all the ingredients together in a heatproof bowl.
2. You want it to be slightly runny so you can drizzle easily over the cookies, so add a splash more water if needed.

Nut and Cranberry Chocolate Slice

As delicious as a block of good-quality dark chocolate is, you can make it even more special by adding your own nuts and berries. You can use any combination of nuts and dried fruits you like but here we've used macadamia and dried cranberries.

Ingredients:
- 200 g/7 oz 70% dark chocolate
- 1 heaped tablespoon of honey
- 2 tablespoons of macadamias, chopped
- 2 tablespoons dried cranberries

Method:
1. Melt chocolate by placing in a heatproof bowl, and placing the bowl over a saucepan of simmering water.
2. Line a small tray with baking paper.
3. Stir honey into the melted chocolate and then pour the chocolate mixture into the tray.
4. Sprinkle nuts and fruit over the chocolate. You can press them gently into the chocolate if you need to.
5. Cover and refrigerate until set.

Pecan Tartlets

These are one of my favourite little cheats, as if you buy a pack of quality tart cases, you simply fill them but they look and taste as if they've taken hours to assemble. We've filled ours with a pecan and maple syrup mix but other delicious, easy-to-make fillings include ricotta and honey, lemon curd, blueberry jam and caramel.

Ingredients:

80 ml/2 ¾ fl oz maple syrup
60 ml/2 fl oz coconut oil
1 tablespoon vanilla extract
2 tablespoons milk
1 tablespoon plain flour
½ cup of pecans, finely chopped
Extra whole pecans for decoration, one per tartlet
24 mini sweet shortcrust tart cases

Method:

1. Melt maple syrup, coconut oil and vanilla in a medium sized saucepan over a medium heat. Bring to the boil and then reduce heat and stir constantly for 5 minutes. Remove from heat and allow to cool.
2. Meanwhile, whisk together the milk and flour and set aside.
3. Pop the pecans under the grill for a minute or two, until lightly toasted.
4. Stir nuts and milk mixture into the maple syrup mixture. Spoon into the tart cases and then top each tart with a single pecan.
5. Cook in a moderate oven for 8–10 minutes.

Orange Cake

This superbly moist cake is decadently delicious but still feels positively healthy to eat thanks to all the oranges and eggs. It's also handy for when you have gluten-free friends popping over for afternoon tea.

Ingredients:

2 large oranges
5 eggs
220 g/7 oz raw sugar
¼ teaspoon bicarbonate of soda (baking soda)
200 g/6 ½ oz almond meal

Method:

1. Simmer whole oranges for 2 hours, topping up with water now and then to keep them covered. Once cooked, allow to cool a little before removing the cores and seeds. Pop oranges (including their skins) in a blender or food processor and puree.
2. Preheat oven to 180°C/350°F.
3. Beat eggs and sugar until light and creamy.
4. Sift the bicarbonate of soda into the almond meal and mix well.
5. Fold all the ingredients together before pouring into a greased 20 cm/8 in springform tin.
6. Bake for one hour or until a skewer inserted into the centre comes out clean. Remove from the oven and allow to cool in the tin.
7. Decorate with a dusting of icing sugar and fresh flowers.

Tip: you can cook extra oranges if you like and freeze for later use.

Nana's Chocolate Cake

There are many delicious chocolate cake recipes out there that require expensive ingredients such as almond meal and bars of dark chocolate. What I like about my nana's chocolate cake recipe is that it's just made with everyday ingredients you're bound to have in your pantry anyway, such as flour and cocoa powder.

Though it's inexpensive to make, it's utterly delicious and looks especially divine sprinkled with edible flower petals, which are available from specialist delicatessens and supermarkets.

Ingredients:
125 g/4 oz butter
225 g/7 oz sugar
2 free-range eggs
1 teaspoon vanilla essence
1 teaspoon of bicarbonate of soda (baking soda)
250 ml/8 ¾ fl oz milk
300 g/10 oz plain flour
2 tablespoons cocoa powder
2 teaspoons of baking powder
A pinch of salt

Method:
1. Preheat oven to 180°C/350°F.
2. Cream butter and sugar. Add eggs and vanilla and beat well.
3. Mix the bicarbonate of soda and milk together and set aside.
4. Add the remaining dry ingredients to the butter mixture, using a wooden spoon to mix together.
5. Now add the bicarbonate of soda and milk, and mix well.
6. Pour mixture into a 20 cm/8 in lined cake tin and bake for 30 minutes. Allow to cool a little before turning out onto a wire rack to cool completely.

For Chocolate Icing:
175 g/6 oz butter
3 tablespoons of boiling water
300 g/10 oz icing sugar (powdered sugar)
5 tablespoons cocoa powder
1 teaspoon of vanilla essence

To Make Chocolate Icing:
1. Simply place all the ingredients into a heatproof bowl and stir. Add more boiling water if mixture is too dry, and more icing sugar if mixture is too wet.
2. Once you have the right consistency, pour the icing over your chocolate cake, smoothing with a spatula if necessary.

Ginger Anzac Biscuits

This is just a gingery twist on an Australian favourite. The heat of the ginger really adds to the flavour and it turns the colour of the biscuit a little darker, which I think is nice.

Women used to bake these biscuits to send to the Australian and New Zealand troops during the First World War. As the biscuits needed to be long lasting, they didn't contain eggs — which makes them handy for those times you don't have any eggs left in the fridge.

Ingredients:
150 g/5 oz plain flour, sifted

95 g/3 oz rolled oats

85 g/3 oz shredded coconut

2 tablespoons ground ginger

60 g/2 oz raw sugar

A pinch of salt

60 ml/2 fl oz honey

125 g/4 oz butter, cubed

1 teaspoon of bicarbonate of soda (baking soda)

2 tablespoons boiling water

Method:
1. Preheat oven to 160°C/325°F.
2. Place the flour, oats, coconut, ginger, sugar and salt into a large bowl and mix together. Make a well in the centre.
3. Melt the honey and butter over a low heat. Meanwhile, dissolve the bicarbonate of soda in the boiling water and then add to the honey mixture. It will foam a little.
4. Pour the honey mixture into the well and stir until combined.
5. Drop tablespoons of the mixture onto lined baking trays and bake in a moderate oven for around 15 minutes or until golden brown. Allow to cool on a wire rack.

Cheese Sables

Even for those of us who have a very sweet tooth, it's probably a good idea to add a few savouries to the table — and what better way than by a biscuit. I'm not sure I know anyone who doesn't love these little sables. Traditionally they're served with champagne, but they're just as delicious with a pot of tea.

Ingredients:
100 g/3.5 oz butter, chilled
   and cubed
150 g/5 oz plain flour
1 cup Parmesan cheese

Method:
1. Mix all ingredients together in a food processor or by hand. If mixing by hand, place all ingredients in a bowl and simply use your fingers to rub together until a dough starts to form.
2. Place dough on a lightly floured surface and knead for a minute before dividing in half, and rolling out into two logs. Wrap your logs in cling wrap and refrigerate for 1 hour.
3. Preheat oven to 180°C/350°F.
4. Slice your logs into 1 cm/½ in biscuits and place on lined baking trays.
5. Bake for 15 minutes or until golden brown. Place on a wire rack to cool.

Berries and Cream

Such a simple dish to serve but such a lovely way to add some fresh summer berries to the table. Cream is delicious as is of course, but to make it extra special add a subtle touch of flavour by whisking in a splash of orange blossom or rosewater.

Use thickened cream as it's best for whipping — not double cream, as if it's whipped too furiously it will produce butter — and be conservative when adding the flavour; you only need a few teaspoons of juice and even less if you're using rosewater, as it tends to be quite strong.

Tip: If you don't have orange blossom or rosewater in the pantry, simply try squeezing in a little mandarin or orange juice instead.

CREDITS

Fabric credits: No-zip cushion with flange: 'Cameroon' in Silt by Mokum
Linen curtain: 'Kyoto' in Ginger by James Dunlop Textiles
Sheer curtain: 'Mendil' in Liquorice by Mokum
Pillowcase: 'Mitsi' in Grey by Liberty of London
Fabric lampshade: 'Feathers' in Linen by Catherine Martin by Mokum
Upholstered bedhead: 'Petit Trianon' in Pearl by Mokum

Additional fabric credits: Curtain, page 111: 'Liaison' by Christian Fischbacher with ruffle in 'Vernon' in Citron by James Dunlop
Armchair slipcover, page 13 and bottom right page 21: 'Heron' in Ginger by James Dunlop
Armchair slipcover, pages 20–21 and bedhead, pages 2 and 28: 'Trumpetta' in Taupe by Bianca Lorenne
Cushions, page 16, bottom left: 'Sinhala' in Sky by Schumacher
Cushions, pages 40–41: 'Chamonix' by Christian Fischbacher

Wallpaper credits: How to wallpaper: 'Splendour' in Champagne by Catherine Martin by Mokum

Additional wallpaper credits: 'Perroquet' in black by Nina Campbell, page 27
'Splendour' in Champagne by Catherine Martin for Mokum, pages 82–83
Vintage-inspired digital wallpaper by Flock Creative, page 114

Paint credits: How to paint timber furniture: Murobond PURE Aqua Satin in Breeze
How to 'age' timber furniture: Murobond PURE Chalk Paint in Just White and Snowdrop
How to 'age' metal furniture: Murobond Rust Paint
How to paint walls: Murobond Aqua Satin in Snowdrop

Art credits: Page 20: 'Sanctum' by Lisa Taylor King
Page 115: 'Damask Rose' by Lisa Taylor King
Pages 74, 100 and 101: Illustrations by Saska Scoon

ACKNOWLEDGEMENTS

With heartfelt thanks…

To John Downs for the lovely photography (and for helping me cart props all over the city). To my beautiful daughter Sassie for her baking, illustrating and perfect posing, her gorgeous godmother, designer KT Doyle for her invaluable sewing help (and to Marina and Suzanne) and to Cassie for her orange cake recipe. To all the generous homeowners who allowed us into their homes and gardens; to Liz, Lorena and the team at New Holland; and to my littlest models Olivia, Sienna, Luci and Scarlett.

I'd also like to thank all the wonderful businesses who helped us with props, products and/or locations including Mokum Fabrics, Murobond Paints, Dyman Foams, Lincraft, Bianca Lorenne, Blake and Taylor, Sachs and Cornish, Vintage Frills, The Gatehouse at Glenloch, Lisa Taylor King Gallery and Wild at Heart Flowers. Your generosity is very appreciated.

First published in 2017 by New Holland Publishers
London • Sydney • Auckland
The Chandlery 50 Westminster Bridge Road London SE1 7QY United Kingdom
1/66 Gibbes Street Chatswood NSW 2067 Australia
5/39 Woodside Ave Northcote, Auckland 0627 New Zealand

www.newhollandpublishers.com

ISBN: 9781742578408
Group Managing Director: Fiona Schultz
Publisher: Diane Ward
Project Editor: Liz Hardy
Designer: Lorena Susak
Cover Design: Lorena Susak
Production Director: James Mills-Hicks
Printer: Times Printers

10 9 8 7 6 5 4 3 2 1

Keep up with New Holland Publishers on Facebook www.facebook.com/NewHollandPublishers